MW00774022

Praise for *Plan Red: China's Project to Destroy America*

"China is attacking America. The assault is malicious and relentless. Gordon Chang's *Plan Red: China's Project to Destroy America* not only sounds the critical alarm but also makes clear what the United States must do to defend freedom."

—Lou Dobbs, host of *Lou Dobbs Tonight* and *New York Times* bestselling author of *The Trump Century*

"Gordon Chang's *Plan Red* lays out in precise detail how China plans to bring down America and rule the world. Chang's prescient warning is a wake-up call that we ignore at our peril . . . and our demise."

—KT McFarland, former deputy national security advisor, Department of Defense Distinguished Service Award recipient, and *Wall Street Journal* bestselling author of *Revolution*

"Nobody outside China's political orbit understands Beijing's plans and ambitions better than Gordon Chang. He is the go-to guy to keep current on what is really going on. His integrity and independence make him a national treasure."

—Dick Morris, host of *Dick Morris Democracy* on Newsmax TV and #1 *New York Times* bestselling author of *The Return: Trump's Big 2024 Comeback*

"America may have won the Cold War against the Soviet Union, but Communism is stronger than ever thanks to Beijing and its agents and sympathizers across U.S. campuses, boardrooms, and even inside Congress. One man who fearlessly tells the truth about the greatest threat we face is Gordon G. Chang. Read this book. Before it's too late."

—Sebastian Gorka, PhD, former strategist to President Donald J. Trump and host of Newsmax's *The Gorka Reality Check*

"Gordon Chang's most recent book about communist Chinese anti-American agendas differs from most such warnings, in that he chronicles a sustained and holistic effort to attack, both psychologically and materially, the United States from the inside. And what he outlines is terrifying, from Chinese efforts to poison American youth with fentanyl across an open border and support for organized criminal gangs to operating leaky bio-labs inside the United States. Chang offers a comprehensive account of the Wuhan lab's birth of the COVID-19 virus—and the CCP's efforts to disguise that fact. A much needed wake-up call that China assumes that it is open season on Americans at abroad and now at home, in every imaginable fashion."

—Victor Davis Hanson, Hoover Institution senior fellow and *New York Times* bestselling author of *The End of Everything*

PLAN RED

PLAN RED

★

China's Project to Destroy America

GORDON G. CHANG

Humanix Books
www.humanixbooks.com

Humanix Books

Plan Red: China's Project to Destroy America

Humanix Books, P.O. Box 20989,
West Palm Beach, FL 33416, USA
www.humanixbooks.com | info@humanixbooks.com

Cover Image: © Kevin Frayer/Getty Images
Interior Images: © Getty Images

ISBN: 978-1-63006-280-4 (Hardcover)
ISBN: 978-1-63006-281-1 (E-book)

Printed in the United States of America

10 9 8 7 6 5 4 3 2

To America, a great country,
and to Americans, a good people

Contents

There is a Red Storm rising in the East—
and America is already under assault
from the Chinese Communist Party.
—Lou Dobbs

FOREWORD

China, the International Arsonist

China's plan to destroy America first contemplates the destruction of the rest of the world.

Since 2022, Xi Jinping has set a match to three continents. The Chinese leader green-lighted Russia's invasion of Ukraine and is supporting Russia's war with lethal and other assistance. In North Africa, Beijing, in conjunction with partner Moscow, has been fueling insurgencies that resemble wars.

In the Middle East, China is backing Iran's attacks, through terrorist proxies, on Israel and international shipping. "The Middle East, thanks in no small measure to Beijing, is soaked with blood," Jonathan Bass of energy consultant InfraGlobal told me.

What is the most ambitious aggressor in history doing? Xi Jinping, who reveres Mao Zedong, is taking two pages from his hero's "peasant movement" playbook.

First, Mao in 1949 prevailed over his enemy, Chiang Kai-shek's Nationalist government, in the

Chinese Civil War by "encircling the cities from the countryside."

"While in the countryside, the Communist Party mobilized the masses of peasants and established base areas, thus opening up a road of encircling the cities from the rural areas and seizing political power by armed force," states China.org.cn, a Chinese propaganda site, in *An Illustrated History of the Communist Party of China*.

Ukraine, North Africa, and Israel, as Xi's Beijing sees it, are parts of the "countryside" today.

So, what is the "city"?

The Communist Party's main enemy is the United States of America. In short, Xi believes he must disrupt much of the world to get at America.

The second page of Mao's playbook involves the fomenting of "chaos." "Great chaos under heaven achieves great order under heaven," wrote Mao in 1966 to his wife, Jiang Qing, referring to the eventual establishment of worldwide Chinese rule.

Xi Jinping is assaulting the current order, and the razing of societies is just an intermediate step on his road to the complete control of humanity.

Isn't that goal impossible to achieve?

Whether it is or not, Xi is making progress. We can see his initial successes in today's wars.

Many believe that these conflicts are merely "regional."

Today, however, there is no such thing as a "regional" conflict. Because superpower China is fighting either directly or indirectly around the world, every conflict has global implications. China's leader, in short, is an arsonist, setting fires and fueling attacks on civilization with proxy wars.

In the 1930s, separate wars merged into what we now call World War II. The same thing can happen this time, especially because the United States and its partners do not realize the significance of what is occurring and are taking inadequate measures to confront Beijing.

Xi has not been trying hard to hide what he intends to accomplish, talking all the time about the "Chinese dream."

The "Chinese dream," by itself, is supposed to sound benign, but in context it is ominous. Xi has been working to impose on today's world the vision of China's emperors, who believed they had both the right and the obligation to rule what they called *tianxia*, "all under heaven." In short, they considered themselves the world's only legitimate rulers.

This means Xi does not believe that the United States should be considered a sovereign state.

Xi Jinping's reliance on proxies is a sly strategy to slowly bleed America, but it also betrays a weakness. It's clear, at least at this moment, that he is unable to confront the United States directly. His regime, after all, is beset by worsening crises at home.

The core crisis involves the Chinese economy, which is not growing robustly as Beijing claims. It may even be contracting, but in any event it is not expanding rapidly enough to service debt that the regime and its instrumentalities have incurred, especially since the 2008 global downturn. In substance, China is now experiencing a long-delayed crisis.

The other fundamental weakness is demography. The number of people in China peaked in 2021, and the country could lose two-thirds of its population this century.

The Chinese people believe that the Communist Party, caught in the grip of Xi's reversion to totalitarianism, has no solutions to modern-day problems. Many in China have already given up, either dropping out of society or fleeing for the United States and other countries.

Xi Jinping, therefore, must be seeing a closing window of opportunity to accomplish his goals, which means he must be thinking that he has to move soon against the United States. After all, he cannot achieve his dream without first taking down that great democracy.

China's leader, I believe, realizes that he must make his crisis America's crisis. That is why his regime has a plan to destroy America.

Gordon G. Chang
May 2024

INTRODUCTION

China Is Preparing to Plunge the World Into Conflict

A quarter century ago, General Chi Haotian, China's defense minister and vice chairman of the Communist Party's Central Military Commission, reportedly gave a secret speech advocating the extermination of Americans. His plan was to use disease to clear out the hills, plains, and valleys of North America so that the Chinese people could settle in the vast spaces left uninhabited. "It is indeed brutal to kill one or two hundred million Americans," he said. "But that is the only path that will secure a Chinese century, a century in which the Communist Party leads the world."[1]

The mass murder of Americans is a popular theme in Chinese society. The Communist Party of China, which tightly controls discourse in the People's Republic of China, permits and even encourages incitements to kill Americans. "We are ahead of schedule in terms of overtaking the United States," said prominent Chinese sociologist Li Yi in late 2020 in a public speech, after talking about the devastation caused by COVID-19 to America. "There will be no problem reaching this goal in 2027. The U.S. will not survive." And then he added this, to make clear that he was not merely making a prediction: "As long as we go to work every day, we will drive the U.S. to its death."[2]

The Chinese regime has deliberately killed Americans in great numbers this century—with disease and in other ways—and it has a plan to destroy America. The communist party-state in fact believes it must eliminate the United States to ensure its own survival.

And to accomplish its goals, the regime is now quickly mobilizing to go to war. China is preparing to plunge the world into conflict.

PLAN RED

CHAPTER ONE

Worldwide Chinese Rule

"China is the only country with both the intent to reshape the international order and, increasingly, the economic, diplomatic, military, and technological power to do so," said CIA Director William Burns in July 2023 to an audience in England.[3] So, the ambitions of China's leaders matter.

Xi Jinping wants to shape the world in China's image,[4] and in his conception of the world there is no place for the United States or even the current international order. British leftist Martin Jacques had long recognized that Chinese leaders wanted to radically transform that system. "We stand on the eve of a different kind of world," he wrote in 2009 in *When China Rules the World: The End of the Western World and the Birth of a New Global Order*.[5] "Hitherto, the arrival of a new global hegemon has ushered in a major change in the international order, as was the case with both Britain and then the United States. Given that China promises to be so inordinately powerful and different, it is difficult to resist the idea that in time its rise will herald the birth of a new international order."[6]

Jacques was certainly correct: Chinese ruler Xi Jinping's vision of a strong and dominate state, often expressed as the "Chinese Dream" or the "great rejuvenation of the Chinese nation,"[7] contemplates a radically new system.

Yet, for all the change Xi demands, China's regime portrays itself as benign, a new type of power that is sensitive to the needs of all.[8] Beijing has clothed its intentions in soothing words: China's ruler has continually promoted his "community of common destiny," sometimes rendered as a "community of shared future for all humankind." Xi introduced the concept in late 2012. As the official *China Daily* put it, the idea "epitomizes the direction in which the Chinese government believes global governance should head."[9]

Beijing constantly reinforces its message of change. For instance, "Together for a shared future" was the official motto for the Olympic and Paralympic Winter Games Beijing 2022. Similarly, Chinese propaganda states Xi's Thought on Diplomacy—a "Thought" in Communist Party lingo is an important body of ideological "work"—is "the vision of building a community with a shared future for mankind."[10]

Yet, Beijing's bland-sounding statements about the new international order clothe the Communist Party's broadest and most dangerous ambition: rule of the entire world. Xi Jinping has continually alluded to his expansive goals. His motto for the 2008 Summer Olympics in Beijing was "One World, One Dream."[11] When viewed in the context of his Chinese Dream, the motto suggests that the ambitions of China's leaders are all-encompassing, because they equate Chinese dreams with world ones.

"Some PRC scholars have declared that now is the time for China to be the destined world leader to reorganize the world as one, to turn the China Dream into the World Dream," writes Fei-Ling Wang, the author of *The China Order: Centralia, World Empire, and the Nature of Chinese Power.*[12]

Even the generous-sounding "shared" appears to be code for the acceptance of China's vision by all on the planet. The 2008 Olympic motto, promoting a one-world theme, echoed the view that Chinese emperors had the Mandate of Heaven to rule *tianxia*, "all under heaven."

Xi, since becoming China's ruler in late 2012, when named as the Communist Party's general secretary, has employed direct *tianxia* language. "The Chinese have always held that the world is united and all under heaven are one family," he proclaimed in his 2017 New Year's Message.[13]

His revolutionary message has been explained by the writings of subordinates. For instance, in September 2017, Foreign Minister Wang Yi wrote in *Study Times*, the Central Party School's influential newspaper, that Xi Jinping's "thought on diplomacy has made innovations on and transcended the traditional Western theories of international relations for the past 300 years."[14]

Wang, with his time reference, is almost certainly pointing to the Peace of Westphalia of 1648, the two treaties that ended the Thirty Years' War and established the current international order of separate sovereign states. Wang's use of "transcended," consequently, suggests that Xi wants a world without sovereign states—or at least no more than one of them. The Communist Party now devotes resources to the study of *tianxia*, and its house scholars produce speeches, articles, and essays advocating the imperial conception of the world.

If Wang's message was not clear enough, Xi Jinping eliminated any ambiguity about Chinese ambition. In his July 1, 2021 speech marking the 100th anniversary of the founding of the Communist Party, he proclaimed: "The Communist Party of China and the

Chinese people, with their bravery and tenacity, solemnly proclaim to the world that the Chinese people are not only good at taking down the old world, but also good at building a new one."[15]

A "new one"? China, it is now evident, does not want to live within the current Westphalian system or even to adjust it. Its leaders have proclaimed that they want to replace the rules-based order altogether. Chinese words in this context, therefore, have an ominous tone. In short, Xi Jinping is signaling that he will try to do away with what is seen as Westphalia's cacophony with *tianxia*'s orderliness.

"Harmony" was a favorite term during the era of Hu Jintao, Xi's immediate predecessor, and it has come to mean, to Chinese rulers, complete obedience to their dictates. Xi Jinping has continued the emphasis. "Harmony is the most precious," the official Xinhua News Agency proclaimed in July 2023 in a major statement titled "China's Worldview Rooted in Ancient Civilization."[16]

The harmony and *tianxia* concepts can be traced far back in Chinese thought. Their justification was simple: Just as there is only one sun in the sky and only one father in a family, so there could be only one ruler on earth. "All political power and all judicial verdicts must come from a singular source of the son of heaven, just like all light of life comes from a single sun," writes Wang, also a professor at the Georgia Institute of Technology.[17] Accordingly, China's emperors, obsessed with avoiding division, sought as their ultimate objective a "Grand Unification" of the world[18] or *da tong*, "Great Unity."

"China was the center of its own hierarchical and theoretically universal concept of order," noted Henry Kissinger in *World Order*.[19] "China considered itself, in a sense, the sole sovereign government of the world" with the emperor, "a figure of cosmic dimensions," being the one and only link "between the human and the divine."[20]

According to this view of the universe, foreign societies were subordinate, in varying degrees, to the Chinese emperor, to whom they were obligated to pay tribute. Other rulers, even in faraway lands beyond the effective rule of the emperor, were necessarily considered transitory and illegitimate. Despite two intervals during the two millennia of the imperial era, China's totalitarian *tianxia* system was the basis of Chinese rule, and it is still the basis of rule, even during the proclaimed communism of the People's Republic of China.

China's leaders see the world as theirs—and theirs alone—because, among other things, they have trouble cooperating with other states. "In all of China's extravagant history," Kissinger wrote in *On China*, "there was no precedent for how to participate in a global order, whether in concert with—or opposition to—another superpower."[21]

There is no "cultural DNA"[22] that forces today's Chinese to view the world as emperors did long ago, but the tributary system nonetheless presents, as Stephen Platt of the University of Massachusetts points out, "a tempting model for the country's current leaders—a nostalgic 'half-idealized, half-mythologized past.' "[23]

Is this nostalgic idea of worldwide Chinese rule ludicrous? Yes, but Xi Jinping has even gone one giant step beyond Planet Earth. Chinese officials now consider near heavenly bodies as part of the People's Republic. "The universe is an ocean, the moon is the Diaoyu Islands, Mars is Huangyan Island," said Ye Peijian, the head of China's lunar exploration program, in 2017.[24]

The Japanese-administered Diaoyu, islets in the East China Sea, are claimed by China, but Tokyo has far stronger legal arguments. Huangyan is Beijing's name for Scarborough Shoal, which China seized from the Philippines in early 2012.

Chinese officials have talked publicly about their territorial designs on space. "If we don't go there now even though we're capable of doing so, then we will be blamed by our descendants," Ye said, referring to the moon and Mars. "If others go there, then they will take over, and you won't be able to go even if you want to."[25]

The name of China's Mars rover, Zhurong, is indicative of Chinese intentions. Xinhua News Agency explained in April 2021 that Zhurong is the god of fire and noted that "Zhu" means "wish," and "rong" translates as "integration."[26] China's official media outlet did not mention, however, that Zhurong is also a god of war. And he is the god of the South China Sea, which Beijing, in violation of its U.N. Convention on the Law of the Sea obligations, claims most of as "blue national soil," in other words, as territorial water. "Zhurong," unfortunately, is a hint that Xi Jinping takes the notion of *tianxia* literally, which makes him the most ambitious aggressor in history.

The implications of Xi's views are, for many, difficult to grasp. What China's ruler is really saying is that no state other than China is sovereign, and so he believes that the United States is merely one of China's colonial possessions, at best a tributary society.

Xi Jinping, therefore, sees a need to undermine every other society, but he knows that his primary—and first—target must be the United States, the guarantor of the international system. America, as Bill Clinton and Madeleine Albright were fond of saying, was and remains "the indispensable nation."[27] American ideals, anathema to China's communist regime, may be compelling for everyone else, but as Fareed Zakaria reminds readers, "they still come wrapped in American power."[28] And it is, therefore, American power that stands in the way of China's realization of its ambitions, at least as the Chinese regime sees them.

Moreover, there is one more reason why Xi Jinping believes he needs to end the existence of the American state. The Communist Party of China, informally the CCP, views the United States as an existential threat not because of anything Americans have ever said or done but because of who they are and what they stand for. An insecure ruling organization in China is afraid of the inspirational impact of America's ideals and form of governance on the Chinese people. This means America's mere existence is considered a direct threat to communist rule. In short, there is nothing Washington can do to achieve stable relations with a Beijing in communist hands.

Chinese hostility to America is, therefore, inherent in the nature of the country's regime. In May 2019, *People's Daily*, the Party's self-described "mouthpiece" and therefore the most authoritative publication in China, carried a landmark editorial declaring a "people's war" on America.[29] This phrase has special meaning. "A people's war is a total war, and its strategy and tactics require the overall mobilization of political, economic, cultural, diplomatic, military, and other power resources, the integrated use of multiple forms of struggle and combat methods," declared a column carried in April 2023 by PLA Daily, an official news website of the People's Liberation Army.[30]

The Party now flaunts its animosity toward the United States. Most of America's political elite have chosen not to see the Chinese regime's antipathy, and those who have noticed dismiss hostile words as mere rhetoric. Unfortunately, the hostility is significant. As James Lilley, Washington's ambassador to Beijing in the late 1980s and early 1990s, memorably said, "the Chinese always telegraph their punches." The Party, with strident anti-Americanism, is establishing a justification to strike America. Beijing has issued malicious propaganda almost every day since the declaration of the people's war.

The Communist Party's malicious assault on America is also a product of the Chinese world view. For millennia—even before the beginning of the imperial era in the third century BC—the notion of struggle for survival has dominated Chinese strategic thinking. This dark vision has been exacerbated by a Communist Party that idealizes not only struggle but also domination and violence, one reason why Party governance has returned to strongman rule under Xi Jinping after decades of attempts to institutionalize internal rules, guidelines, and norms. Xi has reversed what many considered progress toward normalization. His motto, as stated by a political ally, is the Mao-era "You die, I live."[31] It is natural, then, that his external outlook is focused on "struggle."[32]

Xi Jinping's view of the world is especially dark, even for a Chinese leader, as is evident from a series of recent pronouncements to domestic audiences, especially his Work Report, a nearly two-hour speech that opened the 20th National Congress of the Communist Party in October 2022. He outlined then a grim situation, more remarkable because no nation threatened China.

"The CCP sees the U.S. as its 'main enemy'—the *hegemon* to be overthrown so that China can take its rightful place as the new global *hegemon*," Kerry Gershaneck, author of *Political Warfare: Strategies for Combatting China's Plan to "Win Without Fighting,"* told me. "It is *at war* with us to achieve this end."[33]

CHAPTER TWO

China's Plan

Xi Jinping obviously believes that he must destroy America to accomplish his objectives. Does he have a plan to do so?

China's rulers, as good communists, have plans for everything, so of course they have a plan for their most important objective. "I learned that these hawks had been advising Chinese leaders, beginning with Mao Zedong, to avenge a century of humiliation and aspired to replace the United States as the economic, military, and political leader of the world by the year 2049 (the one hundredth anniversary of the Communist Revolution)," Michael Pillsbury, now at the Heritage Foundation, writes. "This plan became known as 'the Hundred-Year Marathon.' It is a plan that has been implemented by the Communist Party leadership from the beginning of its relationship with the United States."[34]

Pillsbury learned of the century-long program from Liu Mingfu, a former Chinese colonel and author of the nationalist book *The China Dream*. Liu, unfortunately, sees conflict with the United States. He called the contest with America "the largest game of global power in human history."[35] His goal, as he put it, is to bring about the "post-American era." [36]

For decades, Americans have had a significantly different view of relations with Beijing, because they have had significantly different views of the arc of historical events. Americans largely accepted the view that their victory in the Cold War was an inflection point of epochal significance. History ended, Francis Fukuyama of Johns Hopkins argued in his landmark 1992 book, *The End of History and the Last Man*. Events continued to occur, he noted, but by the last days of the Cold War "the evolution of human societies through different forms of government had culminated in modern liberal democracy and market-oriented capitalism."[37] Humanity had finally reached the "end point of mankind's ideological evolution."[38]

Americans, therefore, believed that the impersonal forces of history, relentlessly grinding forward, would finish off Chinese communism. China's communists, the victors of the Cold War knew, would soon realize that they were benefiting from the American-dominated international system and would therefore come to support it. The State Department's Robert Zoelleck expressed the mood of the times when in 2005 he talked about China becoming a "responsible stakeholder" in the international system.[39]

Therefore, America had tried to ease China's transition from Marxist economics and Maoist political institutions to free-market ideology and institutions that resembled, at least in broad outline, America's. Washington's policy, the grandest wager in history, turned out to be America's biggest mistake. Yes, inside the existing geopolitical order China prospered. In fact, the people who benefited the most from the American-led system were not the Americans but the Chinese.

Chinese leaders made a show of accepting the world as it was while it was in their interest to do so, and, as a result, the People's Republic, for the first time in its decades of existence, seemed to be working inside the international system. Beijing's diplomats, intending to allay fears, spoke in pleasing tones during this time.

Chinese officials, however, retained ambitions that collided with those of Americans and others. As China grew stronger, its regime did not think it was in its interest to defend the system that had been essential to its rise. Chinese leaders instead believed they had the means to tear down that system and began doing so. All Deng Xiaoping, Mao Zedong's successor, said was that the Chinese should *tao guang yang hui*, often translated as "hide your strength, and bide your time."

That piece of advice came from China's Warring States period, a time that produced numerous proverbs, stories, and maxims about deception. "Chinese strategy is, at its core, a product of lessons derived from the Warring States period," [40] writes Pillsbury.

During the Long March, Mao brought only one book with him, a "statecraft manual" based on the learning of that time.[41]

The Chinese are also fascinated by another treatise of misdirection, cunning, and deception: *The Thirty-Six Stratagems*. "All of these stratagems," Pillsbury notes, "are designed to defeat a more powerful opponent by using the opponent's own strength against him, without his knowing he is even in a contest."[42] "We don't know we are losing the game," he believes. "In fact, we don't even know that the game has begun."[43]

The Chinese did not have to try hard to fool Americans, who were dazzled by Fukuyama and wanted, in any event, to be fooled. American policymakers often refused to notice Chinese hostility. When the Chinese regime behaved poorly,

American leaders were patient, indulgent, and forgiving. President Joe Biden's comments minimizing the Chinese spy balloon, which surveyed sensitive military sites in the United States in January and February 2023,[44] show that even today the American policymaking community has great tolerance for belligerent Chinese conduct.

The balloon incident shows Beijing's utter disrespect for the United States, an attitude it openly displayed when China's top two diplomats traveled to Alaska to meet Secretary of State Antony Blinken and National Security Advisor Jake Sullivan at the now-famous showdown in Anchorage in March 2021.

"So, let me say here that, in front of the Chinese side, the United States does not have the qualification to say that it wants to speak to China from a position of strength," said China's top diplomat, Yang Jiechi, as part of a long tirade. His words were immediately amplified by Chinese state and Communist Party media, carried for weeks, first by reporting and then by analyses. Yang's initial rant and its coverage were planned well in advance in a tactically brilliant and seamless operation.

Yang's storyline was especially heard in Chinese media as Kabul was falling that year, and the troubles afflicting America are propagated virtually every day by Beijing. These days, the Communist Party's regime talks not only about China's rise but also about America's decline. Xi Jinping's narrative is that China is leading the "East." In a landmark speech at the end of 2020, he stated that "the East is rising, and the West is declining."[45]

Xi obviously believes this is the time for China to make its mark. He was not especially subtle on March 22, 2023. "Change is coming that hasn't happened in 100 years," he said to Vladimir Putin in Moscow while bidding farewell after their 40th in-person meeting. Xi then said: "And we are driving this change together."[46]

Xi, in his March 22 comments, essentially announced to the world that China was now in charge and that the United States was no longer a power to be reckoned with. That assessment was arrogant in the extreme, but arrogance is his trademark and the basis of his diplomacy.

And that leads to Xi Jinping's plan for America. He is no longer waiting for 2049, the hundredth anniversary of Communist Party rule, the end of the "marathon" that Liu Mingfu and Michael Pillsbury talk about. Xi is evidently moving now. While America's elite think their country is at peace, China's regime is waging its brand of war.

So, what is the Xi Jinping war plan? The plan is evident from his words, from another hundredth anniversary.

In his landmark address of July 1, 2021, Xi promised to "crack skulls and spill blood" of those standing in the way of China's ambitions. Xi has done so with "unrestricted warfare" tactics. In 1999, two Chinese air force colonels, Qiao Liang and Wang Xiangsui, in *Unrestricted Warfare* advocated the use of any tactics, including terrorism, to take down the United States. That book, in a real sense, is the tactical manual for China's marathon of a hundred years.

CHAPTER THREE

Political Warfare

In 2020, China evidently wanted to unseat President Donald Trump, so it engaged in a massive public diplomacy campaign as well as surreptitious and malicious use of social media. Beijing's anti-Trump effort looked like it exceeded Russian election meddling both that year and in 2016.

In August 2020, Director of National Intelligence John Ratcliffe said that China, engaged in "election influence and interference" and other activities, was the greatest national security threat to America.[47] Beijing that year had issued, in both Chinese state and Communist Party media, propaganda intending to tar the Trump administration. The volume of newspaper stories, social media postings, and pronouncements was unprecedented.

Moreover, the Communist Party's *Global Times*, a tabloid, and the Chinese Foreign Ministry had engaged in apparently coordinated public disinformation campaigns targeting Trump. Two of these campaigns were especially vicious, one over the coronavirus epidemic and the other in connection with the nationwide George Floyd protests.[48] In the later campaign, the Chinese were trying to stoke racial tension.

Moreover, Beijing unleashed its trolls and bots against Trump in a multi-faceted offensive. For instance, the *New York Times* reported that in March 2020 Beijing tried to cause chaos in America by spreading, through text messages and social media feeds, rumors that Trump would invoke the Stafford Act to lock down the entire country. Beijing obviously knew the coronavirus rumors were false.[49]

In addition, as Fox News reported in August of that year, a Chinese operation, dubbed "Spamoflauge Dragon," had been relentlessly attacking Trump and spreading disinformation on a variety of topics.[50] YouTube, Facebook, and Twitter took down its accounts. Twitter and other sites have periodically purged fake Chinese users. In June of that election year, Twitter said it had removed 174,000 of them.[51]

As Paul Dabrowa, an Australian national security expert, wrote in a private note, "weaponized propaganda," especially when powered by artificial intelligence, "can trigger wars, economic collapse, riots, and protests of all kinds." "It can," Dabrowa states, "also destroy the credibility of government institutions and turn a population against itself."[52]

China's campaign against America excludes nothing and uses every point of contact with American society to destroy it. "Communist China's primary means of defeating America is political warfare," Gershaneck, also a NATO fellow for Hybrid Threats, wrote to me. "While it is fair to say that the CCP prefers to win this war *without fighting*, it is more accurate to say the CCP intends to win *without us fighting back*."[53]

The party-state, as a part of its political warfare campaign, has long targeted America's disaffected. "The Communist Party uses 'unrestricted warfare' tactics to create or exacerbate social fragmentation," Cleo Paskal of the Foundation for Defense of Democracies told me. "It is a form of entropic warfare in which the target country is weakened to the point of internal chaos. As institutions, societies, and economies break down, it becomes easier for the CCP's political warfare to be effective in shaping outcomes desired by Beijing."[54]

The Chinese Communists are, as they say, conducting a "smokeless war."[55]

That smokeless war is conducted everywhere, including America's jails. There is no mystery as to who is flooding American prisons with propaganda, specifically Xi Jinping's writings in Spanish. An inmate in the U.S. Penitentiary, Lewisburg, says that someone has been sending to inmates *La Gobernacion y Administracion de China*, the Chinese leader's thoughts about governance and administration.[56]

China's regime has traditionally courted those who seek to disrupt society. Huey Newton, cofounder and leader of the Black Panther Party, visited Mao Zedong's China in 1971 and even was accorded a meeting with Premier Zhou Enlai in the Chinese capital.

As a result of this continual courting, America's militants were inspired by Mao, including the Young Lords, who forcibly seized a hospital in the South Bronx and turned it into a Maoist-inspired "acupuncture collective" with its own Chinese-style "barefoot doctors." The collective helped people kick drug addiction as a means of turning them into "activists." Young Lords cofounder Mickey Melendez explained the importance of using Chinese acupuncture to detox converts: "This brings us all together, this brings our health program together, our politics together, our direct action together."[57] The collective's acupuncturists were involved in radical action, and they read from Mao's *Little Red Book*.

"The Chinese Communist Party openly supported the sort of political activism in the U.S. that would get you sent to a work camp or worse in China," says Paskal. "While those engaging in violence to advocate for minority rights—or who even mentioned minority rights—wouldn't last long in Mao's China, Beijing offered support and guidance to those in the U.S. and elsewhere doing the same."[58]

Recently, China has become bold, openly fomenting violence. On October 18, 2021, Chen Weihua, *China Daily's* European bureau chief, posted a tweet including these words: "Hope there will be more petrol bomb throwing mobs in protests in the U.S."[59] Chen was inciting Americans to violence and, coming from a Chinese official acting in his official capacity, committing an act of war.

For the most part, however, the Communist Party's subversion is not so public. In August 2020, Radio Free Asia reported that a People's Liberation Army intelligence unit, working out of the now-closed Houston consulate, was using big data to identify Americans likely to participate in Black Lives Matter and Antifa protests and then created and sent them "tailor-made" videos on how to organize riots. Related reporting reveals that the videos were distributed by TikTok.[60]

Americans initially focused on Beijing's surreptitious theft of data through the wildly popular mobile video-sharing app. Nonetheless, TikTok's main national security threat involves the distribution of Beijing propaganda: The app is one of the Party's most useful instruments of persuasion.

"TikTok is a powerful tool of national subversion and indoctrination," said Brandon Weichert, an American-based China watcher, to me.[61] TikTok is owned by Chinese company ByteDance, which also owns Douyin, TikTok's sister site in China. Douyin manages TikTok's algorithms, including those that determine which videos are shown to which users. That access gives Beijing the ability to "boost the signal"—curate content with powerful artificial intelligence. Powerful AI can get people to think—and act—in certain ways. TikTok, as a result, delivers, better than any other platform, customized content, which is why it is so addictive—and successful. As Dabrowa told me in the middle of 2020, "My team discovered that TikTok can be used to trigger desired responses and behaviors."[62]

In fact, Beijing has been using TikTok to flood the world with "weaponized propaganda."

"If the CCP can weaponize a balloon, think about what it can do with 150 million American TikTok users at its mercy," Keith Krach, chair, and cofounder of the Krach Institute for Tech Diplomacy at Purdue University, told me.[63]

China uses TikTok to, among other things, weaken America.

How so? For one thing, the app glorifies drug use. Yes, the wildly popular app has community guidelines prohibiting videos promoting illegal drugs, but you can find clips with millions of views teaching kids how to take them.[64]

"TikTok routinely conveys Chinese Communist Party propaganda, while censoring criticism of the People's Republic of China and information the CCP wants suppressed," Gershaneck, the political warfare expert, told me. "It is no surprise, then, that TikTok seems to be actively supporting Russian propaganda and disinformation regarding Putin's rape of Ukraine."[65] TikTok parent ByteDance has signed support agreements with Beijing's security apparatus, Gershaneck reports, and ByteDance boasts of its commitment to promote the Communist Party's agenda. In a sense, all Chinese platforms are suspect. In the Communist Party's top-down system, no company, private or state-owned, can disregard regime dictates.

China's regime has marched TikTok off to war against America. "Through political warfare, the

CCP disarms us intellectually and psychologically as it co-opts, corrupts, and ultimately controls key American elites, particularly political and foreign policy decision makers," says Gershaneck.[66]

Furthermore, Beijing buys Americans of influence. It has almost certainly purchased most of the Biden family. James Biden admitted in February 2024 that he had passed along money he had received from Chinese company CEFC China Energy to his brother Joe Biden in 2017, between his stints as vice president and president.[67]

In March 2023, a spokesperson for Hunter Biden's legal team admitted that the younger Biden had received "good faith seed funds" from "a legitimate energy company in China," presumably CEFC.[68] That was essentially an admission of corruption, because, in the absence of corruption, no Chinese business under these circumstances would pay such a large sum without the recipient being bound by contract.

The Chinese themselves certainly think the Biden family has been purchased. In November 2020, Renmin University's Di Dongsheng gave a lecture publicized widely inside China. Di claimed that China, with Joe Biden in the Oval Office, would control outcomes at the highest levels in Washington, arguing that Beijing could make offers that could not be refused and that every American could be bought with cash. Di got the biggest laugh of the livestreamed lecture when he spoke the four Chinese characters—亨特拜登—that form the name "Hunter Biden."[69]

Disturbingly, the Biden family and TikTok have now become intertwined. Joe Biden's re-election campaign—"Biden HQ"—joined the app, posting a video captioned "lol hey guys" during the Super Bowl in February 2024.[70]

In addition to the Bidens, China has purchased hundreds—if not thousands—of American politicians, academics, businesspeople, and law enforcement officials at the federal, state, and municipal levels.

How do we know the penetration has been so complete? For instance, China's Ministry of State Security first contacted Rep. Eric Swalwell (D-Ca.) not when he was serving on the House Intelligence Committee—where he would be of great value to Beijing—but when he was on the city council of Dublin City, California.[71] Swalwell could not have been the only aspiring politician whom Beijing had been grooming then.

We in fact know that he was not the only one. Swalwell was targeted by Christine Fang, now known to be a Ministry of State Security agent. Fang, also known as “Fang Fang,” was busy, enchanting politicians across the United States before she was withdrawn from the country.

“The Chinese Communist Party uses three color-coded ‘political-interference tactics’ to gain influence over American citizens at home as well as those who naively travel to China,” Charles Burton of Prague-based think tank Sinopsis points out.[72] “Blue refers to sophisticated cyberattacks on target computers, smartphones, and hotel rooms for possible blackmail. Gold refers to bribes, while yellow means ‘honey pots,’ sexual seduction.”

As Burton, a former Canadian diplomat in Beijing, notes, these color-coded tactics “are part of a sophisticated engagement coordinated by the agents of the Communist Party’s massive United Front Work Department working under diplomatic cover at China’s embassies and consulates.”[73]

China’s agents surveil, harass, recruit, blackmail, and intimidate those in America and work out of, among other places, Beijing’s four remaining consulates and the large Washington, D.C., embassy as well as many state banks and enterprises, Confucius Institutes and Confucius Classrooms, and affiliated organizations, such as the Chinese Students and Scholars Association. China’s regime, over the course of decades, has infiltrated just about every organization of influence in the United States.

In short, China has been attacking America from within America.

The attackers these days are not hard to spot, as China's political warfare campaign has become increasingly brazen. The America ChangLe Association in Manhattan's Chinatown, which closed after an FBI raid in 2022, reopened the following year with a grand ceremony celebrating July 4.[74] The raid shut "the first overseas police station in the United States" for the Fuzhou branch of China's Ministry of Public Security. The "clandestine" operation, however, was in fact run by the UFWD, as the United Front Work Department, is commonly known.

It was good that the FBI closed the Chinatown police station, of course, but as Radio Free Asia reports, that station was "a mere sliver of Beijing's U.S. harassment push."[75] For one thing, the UFWD operates "Overseas Chinese Service Centers" in other cities. The Daily Caller News Foundation reports that these OCSCs, as they are called, are in San Francisco, Houston, Omaha, St. Paul, Salt Lake City, St. Louis, and Charlotte.[76] The *New York Post* believes there are other Chinese police stations in New York and Los Angeles.[77]

The UFWD, charged with interfacing with foreign organizations and individuals, often functions as an intelligence service, especially when it operates with the intelligence branches of the People's Liberation Army, another Party organization, and the Chinese central government. The closed New York police station was used as a base targeting those legally in the United States, especially Chinese nationals and American citizens of Chinese descent. It was a breach of China's diplomatic agreements with Washington for Beijing to conduct "law enforcement"—or, for that matter, any other government function—from unannounced locations.

Never has the United States faced such a challenge, and as a result, Americans are now underestimating the danger they face. As Gershaneck warns, "Today, with its modern technology and massive political, military, and economic power, the political warfare of the People's Republic of China presents a totalitarian challenge unprecedented in human history."[78]

China's penetration of American society has been so thorough that the Communist Party has even been able to kill Americans with impunity.

CHAPTER FOUR

Killing Americans

Xi Jinping has committed crimes of the century. His communist regime deliberately spread SARS-CoV-2, the pathogen causing COVID-19, to almost every corner of the planet. Moreover, China's leader has another great crime to account for: the peddling of illicit fentanyl. Both crimes have killed—and are still killing—Americans.

On COVID, China's regime ensured that the disease spread to the wider world. Chinese officials both hid its origins and lied about them. First, Chinese officials have insinuated or outright stated that America, Italy, Spain, or India was the source of the disease. The Party's *Global Times* has even pushed the wacky multiple-origin thesis of Wang Peiyu of Peking University's School of Public Health.[79] Beijing, in addition to promoting baseless theories, announced boldly that COVID-19 started outside China.

By now, the weight of the evidence, both direct and circumstantial, shows that the disease was either engineered or stored at a Chinese biological weapons laboratory, the Wuhan Institute of Virology, in the central city of Wuhan. As time passes, more and more facts point to that institution as the source of the disease.[80]

Beijing has a fundamental problem: It cannot marshal scientific proof for its weird origin theories. "The Communist Party has not provided any evidence of zoonotic transmission of the virus from animal to human for the Wuhan outbreak," Sean Lin, a former lab director of the viral disease branch of the Walter Reed Army Institute of Research, told me. "Bats or pangolins that are potential reservoirs for the virus were identified thousands of miles away from Wuhan. So far, no animal reservoir for the virus has been identified in Wuhan."[81]

Yet, whether SARS-CoV-2 was engineered to be a weapon, Xi Jinping turned it into one by deliberately spreading COVID-19 beyond China's borders. Whenever symptoms first appeared—there is great debate on this point—doctors in Wuhan knew by the second week of December 2019 that the disease was highly contagious. Xi, who runs a totalitarian or near-totalitarian state, had to know soon afterward. Hundreds, if not thousands, were falling ill in that city.

Yet, China did not publicly acknowledge human-to-human transmissibility until January 20 of the following year, when Zhong Nanshan, a famed Chinese pulmonologist, acknowledged two such transmissions in Guangdong province, and China's National Health Commission officially confirmed human-to-human spreading.[82]

In short, for at least five weeks and perhaps for five months, Beijing delayed informing the world. If China had said nothing during this period, its actions would have been grossly irresponsible, but in January 2020 Chinese officials deceived the international community with a false narrative of non-transmissibility. The World Health Organization, in a January 9 statement[83] and January 14 tweet,[84] announced that, based on information from China, the disease was not readily contagious. Chinese health officials told their American counterparts the same thing in private communications.[85]

Moreover, Xi, while locking down Wuhan and surrounding cities where the disease had spread, pressured countries to not impose restrictions and quarantines on arrivals from China. By preventing travel in his own country, he obviously thought such measures were effective in stopping disease, so it's clear that he thought he was spreading the disease by leaning on others, including the United States, to keep borders open to arrivals from China.

Therefore, Xi turned an in-country epidemic into a once-in-a-century pandemic. This is the first time in history that one nation has attacked all the others.

So far, 1.2 million Americans have perished from this disease, according to the COVID Data Tracker of the Centers for Disease Control and Prevention.[86] Xi Jinping is not done killing, however.

China's military is almost certainly working on pathogens that target certain ethnic groups. China's National Defense University, in the 2017 edition of the authoritative *Science of Military Strategy*, mentioned a new kind of biological warfare of "specific ethnic genetic attacks."[87] American officials are concerned that China has been experimenting with such germ weapons, as Bill Gertz of the *Washington Times* has reported.[88] Beijing's relentless efforts to collect genetic profiles of foreigners while preventing the transfer from China of the profiles of Chinese are indications of sinister intentions.

If Chinese scientists succeed in designing pathogens that leave Chinese people alone but sicken only foreigners, the next disease from China could end non-Chinese societies. This will be Communist

China's weapon against the world, the one General Chi Haotian was talking about using.

"The problem with the report of the Chi Haotian speech is that it cannot be verified," Richard Fisher of the International Assessment and Strategy Center said to me. "When it was revealed in 2005, it seemed fantastical that China would unleash biological warfare against the United States to massacre its population and pave the way for a Communist Party invasion, occupation, and exploitation."

Since that time, he points out, Chinese "actions have given that report increasing credibility." Fisher notes that the 2002 outbreak of Severe Acute Respiratory Syndrome, SARS, may have been the result of a leak from a Chinese biological warfare laboratory, and the COVID-19 pandemic almost certainly originated from such a facility. Therefore, "the Chi Haotian speech reads more like a real warning." As Fisher points out, the Communist Party is capable of unfathomable evil, such as the massacre of 300 million Americans."[89] Many analysts have said that bioweapons are not practical, yet COVID-19 has killed millions and hobbled societies around the world. It is the ultimate proof of concept.

Cleo Paskal, the Foundation for Defense of Democracies scholar, told me that "China's

Communist Party uses an empirical framework called Comprehensive National Power, or CNP, to rank countries."

"If Chinese leaders realize they have an epidemic on their hands that will lower China's CNP, it is logical to turn that epidemic into a pandemic by restricting the spread domestically while not stopping the spread internationally," Paskal says. "That way, China's CNP might be lowered, but so will everyone else's, and China's relative ranking won't be affected, in fact, it might even improve."[90] And that is what Beijing undoubtedly did. It spread COVID-19 to decrease the CNP of others in order to achieve its goal of making China the most powerful country on the planet.

Xi Jinping is also killing Americans with fentanyl, one of dozens of opioids that Chinese gangs design and make in their laboratories in China. Yes, Xi in his November 15, 2023 meeting with Biden promised to limit fentanyl sales, but the Chinese leader made the same promise in 2018 to Trump[91] and in 2016 to President Obama.[92]

While China's regime makes promises, it continues to provide subsidies for the production and export of precursor chemicals for fentanyl.[93] Chinese producers and gangs sell the precursors, primarily to the Sinaloa and Jalisco cartels in Mexico. The cartels, with the help of technicians from China, mix the Chinese precursors and then smuggle the fentanyl through a wide-open southern border into the United States, now in record volumes. The result, Vanda Felbab-Brown of the Brookings Institution wrote, is "the deadliest drug epidemic in U.S. history."[94]

Centers for Disease Control and Prevention statistics show that there were approximately 75,000 American deaths attributed to synthetic opioids in 2022. Other estimates are higher. Anthony Ruggiero of the Foundation for Defense of Democracies says this is like suffering a 9/11 every two weeks.[95] Whatever the toll, each person who has perished was the victim of a crime perpetrated by the Communist Party of China.

Why?

The regime knows all the details of the fentanyl trade. As an initial matter, some of the producers of this opioid are state enterprises or state-owned. Yet, the Communist Party is also aware of the activities of the criminal gangs producing fentanyl.

In the past, fentanyl producers sent their product to the United States through China's state postal system. Now, after increased American scrutiny of the mail, they primarily ship by container. Every container leaving China is inspected by officials.

Moreover, the People's Republic of China maintains the world's most sophisticated surveillance state. With the possible exception of the Democratic People's Republic of Korea—North Korea—no state knows more about the activities of its people.

There are in China about 700 million facial recognition surveillance cameras, about one camera for every two residents. Those devices are being connected to one centrally controlled system as the regime stitches together a nationwide social credit system to continuously assess and rank the observable behavior of each and every person in China. In addition, the regime uses 1.76 billion cellphones[96]—almost a billion of which are smartphones—for surveillance purposes. Taxis and other vehicles have government-installed cameras. The Communist Party of China has thought of just about everything.

China is not, as analysts say, "authoritarian." It may not be fully "totalitarian" yet, but in any event, it is quickly becoming a total surveillance state. The Party cannot run such a state and claim that it does not know what is going on. So, the party-state knows what the large, organized criminal gangs have been doing over the course of decades. It's obvious, therefore, that these criminal organizations operate with the knowledge and approval of the party-state.

Moreover, the Chinese surveillance state does more than just know and approve; it gives the gangs support, such as diplomatic cover. In early April 2023, for instance, the Chinese foreign ministry stated: “There is no such thing as illegal trafficking of fentanyl between China and Mexico.”[97]

Furthermore, the gangs launder proceeds through the Chinese state banking system, as do many other criminal elements in the Western hemisphere. Chinese “money brokers” work for Latin American drug gangs and have quickly displaced Mexican and Colombian competitors.

How have the Chinese gangs done that? With Chinese banking apps, for one thing. China’s gangs are moving large sums quickly and quietly with those apps. As a result, they have taken over the movement of dirty cash in Mexico and other countries. For instance, one Chinese ring, based in Guadalajara, worked for the Sinaloa Cartel and other drug gangs. China’s criminals, according to U.S. federal prosecutors, “have come to dominate international money laundering markets.”[98]

No one could launder sums through the Chinese financial system without the knowledge of the Communist Party, especially because the Party tightly controls the banking system. Most of China’s large banks are either wholly or majority-owned by the state. The Party, therefore, is either directly or indirectly responsible for money laundering for Latin America drug gangs—and others.

"One of the prime sources that underwrites their efforts is Chinese money laundering," said Admiral Craig Faller, then commander of U.S. Southern Command, to the Senate Armed Services Committee in March 2021, referring to China.[99]

The Communist Party is using all of its resources to support criminal activity in America, and Americans, as a result, are dying.

China's regime is planning to kill Americans in even greater numbers, however. It is marching the country to war.

CHAPTER FIVE

China's War Plans

Xi Jinping's China is preparing to go to war. Not "unrestricted war" or political war but "hot war" or "kinetic war," in other words, war as Americans see it in the movies.

Xi can't stop talking about going into battle. In 2023, during the National People's Congress annual meeting, he reiterated his favorite phrase: "Dare to Fight."[100] A year later, at the same event, he gave specific directives to the People's Liberation Army and the People's Armed Police about fighting.[101]

Xi is doing more than just talking, however. He is implementing the largest and fastest military buildup since the Second World War, he is trying to sanctions-proof the Chinese regime, he is stockpiling grain and other commodities, he is surveying America for strikes and sabotage, he is mobilizing China's civilians for battle, and he is purging China's military of officers who are opposed to going to war.

It's not hard to figure out who Xi believes is the enemy. For instance, the People's Liberation Army in January and February 2023 surveiled U.S. nuclear weapons sites, including Malmstrom, F. E. Warren, and Minot Air Force Bases, which house all of America's Minuteman III intercontinental ballistic missiles, using a balloon that also passed close by Whiteman Air Force Base, home to the nuclear-capable B-2 bomber fleet, and Offutt Air Force Base, the headquarters of Strategic Command, which controls U.S. nuclear weapons. The flight path showed that China is preparing a nuclear weapons strike on America, perhaps assessing its ability to disrupt the Pentagon's command and control of these weapons.

Moreover, a shower of green lasers over Hawaii on January 28, 2023 was caused by a Chinese satellite.[102] The shower appears to have been an attempt to collect atmospheric data useful for guiding China's hypersonic glide vehicles, which are designed to carry nuclear weapons, to their targets.[103]

Americans should not think war is inconceivable. China's ambitious ruler has already greenlighted one war this decade: Russia's invasion of Ukraine. On February 4, 2022, Xi and Vladimir Putin met in Beijing for the opening ceremony of the Beijing Winter Olympics and issued a 5,300-word statement announcing their "no-limits" partnership. The statement was issued, significantly, just 20 days before Russia attacked Ukraine. Furthermore, Putin waited until just after Beijing's Games to launch his invasion. Since the start of the war, Xi Jinping has given Russia all-in support, including "lethal aid."[104]

Moreover, China has made Tehran's attacks on Israel possible, with elevated purchases of sanctioned oil. Chinese parties took about 90% of Iran's exports of crude in 2023.[105] In addition, Iran's terrorist proxies—Hamas,[106] Hezbollah,[107] and the Houthi militia[108]—all possess large quantities of Chinese weapons, Chinese diplomats support the militant attacks on the Jewish state, and Chinese central government and Communist Party propaganda units amplify Iranian disinformation.

As much as the United States wants to avoid war, China, for a host of internal reasons, is driving hard toward it. And should China ultimately choose war, the United States will almost certainly be in the fight.

Why?

First, Chinese war doctrine is to hit the United States on the first day of fighting. Second, China has been making nuclear weapons threats that could, one way or another, bring the United States into a conflict. Third, China's military is provoking dangerous intercepts with American vessels and aircraft, and these provocative actions will surely escalate. Fourth, China is preparing to fight that war on American soil.

On the first point, China's hostile actions target countries tied to the United States by mutual defense treaties. In the last several years, Beijing has made repeated attempts to seize South China Sea features from the Philippines and East China Sea features from Japan, namely the islets the Japanese call the Senkakus. China has been pressuring South Korea in its exclusive economic zone—the band of territorial water between 12 and 200 nautical miles from a shoreline—and many believe any Chinese attack in East Asia will be supported by a Russian attack on Japan[109] and a North Korean attack on either South Korea or Japan, perhaps both.[110]

An act of war against Japan, South Korea, or the Philippines is an act of war against the United States: The United States has treaty obligations to defend all three states.

The United States is not committed by treaty to defend Taiwan, but an attack on that island republic will almost certainly bring America into the conflict. For one thing, any Chinese invasion of Taiwan will almost certainly be accompanied by acts of war against Japan.

For a Chinese invasion of Taiwan to be successful, China will have to establish a blockade. For that blockade to be successful, it will have to include sovereign Japanese territory, specifically its westernmost inhabited island, Yonaguni, and nearby features. Yonaguni, about 58 nautical miles from the main island of Taiwan, is south of the capital city of Taipei. Taiwan's mountains are visible from the Japanese island on a clear day.

Moreover, Tokyo is supportive of Taipei, because the defense of the Japanese homeland depends on Taiwan remaining in friendly hands. Japan and Taiwan, after all, are part of the same island chain, and Japan's southern flank will be wide open if Taiwan is incorporated by China as its 34th province. As an Asia security expert once told me, "Japan will never let China take Taiwan."

China's military planners know all this, and so their doctrine calls for hitting everybody else first. "In the past and now, Chinese military strategy has stressed overwhelming surprise and preemptive attack," says Richard Fisher, the China military analyst. "When China decides to attack Taiwan with overwhelming force, it will also seek to destroy American and Japanese forces deployed in Japanese bases that could respond to China's attack. They will also likely attack U.S. forces in Guam."[111] Guam is sovereign U.S. territory.

"Commercial satellite imagery from 2013 shows mockups of the U.S. naval base in Yokosuka, Japan, in the test ranges of the PLA's strategic rocket force in central China," notes James Fanell of the Geneva Centre for Security Policy. Fanell, also a former U.S. Navy captain who served as director of Intelligence and Information Operations at the U.S. Pacific Fleet, points out that the U.S. air base in Kadena in Japan and the American military bases in Guam are also targets. Moreover, China is almost certainly thinking of hitting bases in the American homeland. Says Fanell, "Given the expanded operations of the Chinese navy and the improved long-range supersonic, now hypersonic, weapons, U.S. defense planners must consider that Hawaii could be attacked during an invasion of Taiwan."[112]

Second, periodically throughout this century Chinese generals and political leaders have made threats—all unprovoked—to use nuclear weapons against the United States. The most alarming of them were made less than a year after Xi Jinping was first named as Communist Party general secretary.[113] Beijing has also made such threats against American treaty allies Japan and Australia, again without provocation, and it will almost certainly threaten to incinerate any country coming to Taiwan's assistance, as China has made no secret of its plans. For instance, the Chinese Defense Ministry in March 2022 promised "worst consequences" for such aiders.[114]

Beijing apparently believes it can intimidate Washington and others into not getting into a fight, but the threats can also accelerate war by emboldening China into starting hostilities. After all, China's arrogant leaders can miscalculate by thinking their nuke threats will prevent others from joining a war when, for one reason or another, they do not intimidate.

In any event, the ongoing rapid buildup of China's nuclear warheads causes great concern. The Pentagon, in a November 2022 report, forecast that China would quadruple its warheads from about 400 then to 1,500 by 2035. As a part of this effort, China's military has been constructing, in three separate fields in its northern deserts, at least 250 and perhaps as many as 360 silos, which appear designed to take the DF-41 missile. A DF-41 has a maximum range of 9,300 miles, putting all of America in range from those three locations. Moreover, each of these missiles can carry, some assess, 10 warheads. Fisher believes that China is contemplating an even faster buildup of its nuclear arsenal, estimating that it could have between 4,200 and 8,000 warheads by 2035.[115]

"For decades, they were quite comfortable with an arsenal of a few hundred nuclear weapons, which was fairly clearly a second-strike capability to act as a deterrent," Secretary of the Air Force Frank Kendall stated in testimony in March 2023, referring to China. "That expansion that they're undertaking puts us into a new world that we've never lived in before, where you have three powers—three great powers, essentially—with large arsenals of nuclear weapons."

This rapid expansion of the arsenal suggests that China is thinking of first strikes with nukes, as Chinese officials, both in and out of uniform, have threatened throughout this century. "I don't think I've seen anything more disturbing in my career than the Chinese ongoing expansion of their nuclear force," Kendall also testified.[116]

Third, war can start with what appears to be an "accident." On May 26, 2023, a Chinese J-16 fighter dangerously intercepted a U.S. Air Force RC-135 in international airspace over the South China Sea, crossing in front of the American plane and forcing it to fly through the J-16's wake of turbulence. The event took place on the one-year anniversary of China's exceedingly dangerous intercept of a Royal

Australian Air Force P-8 reconnaissance aircraft over the same body of water. That plane, according to the Australian Department of Defense, was engaged in "routine maritime surveillance activity."

The Chinese high-performance aircraft, Australia said, "accelerated and cut across the nose of the P-8, settling in front of the P-8 at very close distance." Then, the Chinese fighter "released a bundle of chaff, which contains small pieces of aluminum, some of which were ingested into the engine of the P-8 aircraft." The Chinese aircraft also fired flares as it was releasing the chaff, metal-coated filament used to confuse radar. This is thought to be the first time any military had used chaff and flares in this manner.[117]

The "chaffing" of the Australian P-8 might have resulted in catastrophe. "Chaff clouds ingested into the P-8's two engines could have caused an inflight emergency and the deaths of the aircrew," Fanell said at the time. Fortunately, the Australian plane, a modified Boeing 737, was able to return to base. China's flying was intentional and of the type likely to damage the P-8, which is in fact what happened. Its actions, therefore, constituted an act of war, as Fanell believes.[118] An act of war against Australia is an act of war against the United States as they are parties to a mutual defense treaty.

China has engaged in a series of troubling intercepts of other aircraft in recent years. In 2018, for instance, the PLA "lit up" a U.S. Air Force C-130 with lasers from China's military base in Djibouti. The action injured two pilots. Fortunately, they were eventually able to land.[119]

These incidents and others evoke the April 1, 2001 collision of a Chinese F-8 fighter jet and a propeller-driven U.S. Navy EP-3 in international airspace over the South China Sea. The Chinese jet, in a reckless maneuver, clipped the wing of the slow-moving EP-3, resulting in the death of the fighter pilot and the U.S. Navy plane making an emergency landing at a Chinese base on Hainan Island. In clear violation of American sovereignty, China's military stripped the American plane of its electronic equipment and held the crew of 24 for 11 days.

Many worry that there will be war if one of these dangerous Chinese aerial intercepts results in another "accident." As a practical matter, there is no such thing as "accidental contact" when it comes to China. There will be such contact if the Chinese military wants such an incident, and there will be no accident if it doesn't. American administrations have continually sought to establish channels of communication to be used in crises, but they are essentially useless. China will talk only when it wants to.

Fourth, China's war plans almost certainly contemplate taking the fight to America in America. In March 2023, for instance, California state and Fresno County officers raided an "unlicensed laboratory" in the city of Reedley and found evidence suggesting a biological warfare campaign. The lab was run by Chinese individuals fronting for parties in China. The FBI and CDC later joined the investigation.

The facility contained lab mice—773 live and more than 175 dead—that were genetically engineered to carry disease. Authorities also found medical waste and chemical, viral, and biological agents. There were onsite at least 20 potentially infectious pathogens, including those causing HIV, hepatitis, herpes, and Ebola.[120]

The lab was supposed to be producing COVID-19 and pregnancy tests,[121] but the facility contained items inconsistent with that explanation. The items seized strongly suggest that China's regime is preparing to spread disease in America, presumably in the months before a war.[122]

"This kamikaze lab—unsecured, poorly contained, makeshift, containing a couple dozen pathogens near a population center—cannot be a one-off,"

Brandon Weichert, author of *Biohacked: China's Race to Control Life*, said to me. "It is, I believe, a part of a large Chinese military operation to spread disease throughout the American population."

"The idea, apparently, is to inhibit Washington's response to a Chinese attack in Asia," said Weichert. "The lab near Fresno, I think, is just the first to be discovered. There must be many more Fresnos out there."[123]

So, will China fire its first shot in the next war from these labs? Probably, but there is already a China-led invasion of the U.S. homeland. "The jungle is filled with Chinese marching to America," said veteran war correspondent Michael Yon to me in June 2023.[124] The most rapidly growing migrant group is from China, with the number of Chinese apprehended at the U.S. southern border in 2023 up 50-fold from two years earlier.[125]

Many of the Chinese migrants are desperate, seeking a better life for themselves and their children. Some, however, are coming to commit acts of sabotage.

Among the arrivals are members of the People's Liberation Army. Representative Mark Green (R-Tenn.), chairman of the House Homeland Security Committee, said at a press conference on June 14,

2023, that, based on his conversation with a Border Patrol sector chief, some of the Chinese migrants at the southern border have "known ties to the PLA." "We have no idea who these people are, and it's very likely, using Russia's template of sending military personnel into Ukraine, China is doing the same into the United States," said Green.[126]

There is almost no question that China's PLA is inserting operatives through the Darien Gap, which separates Colombia from Panama, and then to America's border with Mexico. "At the Darien Gap, I have seen countless packs of Chinese males of military age, unattached to family groups, and pretending not to understand English," said Yon, the correspondent. "They were all headed to the American border."[127]

"Normally in groups of five to fifteen, they typically emerge from the Darien Gap and spend one night in the U.S.-funded San Vicente Camp, or next door in the Tonosi Hotel, before boarding luxury buses for the trip up Highway 1 toward Costa Rica," Yon reports. "One group of six young men bought a chicken at the Tonosi Hotel, drank its blood from small glasses, then cooked the chicken themselves in the hotel restaurant, according to the hotel manager. Drinking raw chicken blood is a rite among some PLA soldiers."[128]

Even more disturbing are recent Chinese migrants—some in the United States for less than three weeks—taking target practice. Videos posted on DefiantAmerica.org in January 2024 depict a sandy location where recent arrivals were sharpening their shooting skills with pistols. One video shows a woman firing a rifle with a scope.[129]

Blaine Holt, a retired U.S. Air Force general, told me in February 2024 that Chinese migrants have been taking target practice in his home state of Idaho, too. "Tens of thousands of military-age men have come across our border and are now in America, organized by group and nationality," Holt said. "Among them are terrorist and state actors, in particular, members of the People's Liberation Army of China. As we speak, these actors are training, making plans and obtaining weapons, watching our patterns, and learning our vulnerabilities."

"We are vulnerable to attack," Holt added. "Our enemies eagerly wait."[130]

Once here, the military fighters can link up with China's agents who are already in place.[131] The concern is that, on the first day of war in Asia, these agents will take down America's power lines, poison reservoirs, assassinate officials, start wildfires, spread pathogens, and create terror by bombing shopping malls and supermarkets.

Furthermore, the saboteurs, China's shock troops, will almost certainly attack American military bases. China has already been probing sensitive installations. Chinese agents posing as tourists have, for instance, intruded into bases, including the Army's Fort Wainwright in Fairbanks, Alaska. There, the suspected Chinese agents drove past a base gate and were later apprehended with a drone inside their car.[132] There is also a report that two Chinese migrants were detected under water surveying a ship in an American port with sonar.

"Ancient Chinese strategists prized the use of subterfuge and surprise to achieve victory, and the two PLA colonels who wrote *Unrestricted Warfare* in 1999 were full of praise for the tactics of Osama bin Laden," Richard Fisher told me.[133] The next war will be fought on American soil with civilians, among others, as targets.

CONCLUSION

What America Must Do Now

China has a plan to destroy America. Does America have a plan to defend itself?

Americans, in the triumphalist mood after the fall of the Soviet Union, thought they should establish extensive contacts with China. Now, the Chinese regime uses these linkages against America and is overwhelming American institutions. The FBI is being overwhelmed, local law enforcement is being overwhelmed, governments at all levels are being overwhelmed, and private organizations are being overwhelmed. As Di Dongsheng, the Shanghai academic, openly boasted in November 2020, China essentially owns Americans and America.[134] "We have people at the top," he bragged. "At the top of America's core inner circle of power and influence, we have our old friends."[135]

After more than three decades of intensive "engagement," it is clear that Washington's generous approach has failed. America has not changed China's regime, as everyone now realizes; China's regime has changed America.

In this situation, there is only one solution: The U.S. needs to sever virtually all points of contact with the regime. Too many Americans now have an interest in supporting the Communist Party. Even billionaire Elon Musk, who loves to talk about freedom while he is in America, bends the knee to China: His Tesla in July 2023 signed a pledge, after a Communist Party demand, to promote "core socialist values."[136] As Oren Cass and Gabriela Rodriguez wrote in *Foreign Affairs* that month, "The United States must break from China or else become irrevocably corrupted by it." As they correctly argue, "De-risking is not enough." There must be a "hard break from China."[137]

Yes, there must be. As an initial matter, Americans must deny Chinese wrongdoers the safe havens and support networks they now enjoy in America. China's principal safe heavens there are its diplomatic compounds. It's time, therefore, to strip the embassy down to the ambassador, family members, and personal staff and close the consulates outright. Also on the chopping block should be all other outposts of the Communist Party, commercial and otherwise. All other Chinese mechanisms of control, such as the Chinese Students and Scholars Association, must be disbanded. In short, everything connected to the regime should be cleared out. Americans cannot afford to leave any Communist Party member or any Chinese saboteur, operative, agent, official, banker, researcher, teacher, or corporate officer in place in America.

As FBI Director Christopher Wray told the American people, "China is engaged in a whole-of-state effort to become the world's only superpower by any means necessary," so "we need a whole-of-society response" to China.[138]

Why should Americans ever allow, as they do now, China to maintain bases in America to attack the American homeland?

More fundamentally, it is time to take a page from Reagan's playbook and work to bring down our enemy: the Communist Party of China. The Party often talks about "win-win" solutions, but as its actions make clear, it believes there can be only one survivor: either the People's Republic of China or the United States of America.

The regime is particularly vulnerable at this moment. Xi himself must be seeing a closing window of opportunity to achieve what he considers are historic goals. In fact, Xinhua News Agency in 2020 ran a piece titled "Xi Stresses Racing Against Time to Reach Chinese Dream."[139]

The situation has deteriorated since then, especially as it became evident in 2023 that the country has not been able to recover from COVID-19. The regime at home is beset by simultaneous crises: continuing debt defaults, accelerating capital flight, a falling currency, crumbling property prices, worsening food shortages, a deteriorating environment, and failing local governments.

Two problems are especially acute. First, the Chinese economy, once the motor of the country's spectacular rise, is now in severe distress. China boomed when Deng Xiaoping, Mao Zedong's successor, allowed liberalization of the state-controlled economic system in the three-decade reform era.

This relaxation, however, was merely a tactical retreat. Deng retained state control of the largest enterprises and banks, and now Xi Jinping is tightening the Party's grip and preventing the further liberalization that must occur if the economy is to become sustainable. Xi will not allow economic liberalization to weaken state institutions, especially the banks, because they help keep the Party in power.

Second, there is demography, the "relentless maker and breaker of civilizations." China stands on the edge of the sharpest demographic decline in history in the absence of war or disease. At the end of this century, the country will, in all probability, be about one-third as populous as it is now. Government efforts to arrest the decline—Beijing moved from a one-child policy in 2015 to a three-child policy in 2021, for instance—have not slowed the relentless fall in birth rates.[140] The country's population peaked in 2021.

Unfortunately for the Chinese regime, Xi reveres Mao and is marching China back to Maoism. He is reinstituting totalitarian social controls, demanding absolute political obedience from everyone, and cutting foreign links. Closing China off from the world is an essential element of his plan to save the communist system. His isolationism and xenophobia evoke policies from the earliest years of the People's Republic and during the two millennia of imperial rule. Every time Chinese leaders have closed off China in this fashion, economic and societal failure soon followed.

Without liberalization of the economy and society, Xi is killing the individual initiative that has made China successful before. And without the perception of societal fairness and safeguards like the rule of law, it's clear that the country has progressed as far as it can within its communist framework. China's current economic difficulties, therefore, are not cyclical but structural.

"China is at the edge of a cliff," says Peter Huessy of GeoStrategic Analysis, accurately summarizing the situation.[141]

The Chinese people know what is wrong and are now angry. Since October 2022 and continuing into the early days of the following year, there was a series of extraordinary protests in China. These demonstrations—some of them large—occurred without coordination, leadership, or organization and showed that Chinese society is particularly volatile. During one of these nationwide outbreaks—in Shanghai, in November 2022—protesters chanted, "Down with Xi Jinping!" and "Down with the Communist Party!"[142]

Revolutionary sentiment is not the Communist regime's only societal concern. There is, for instance, extreme pessimism in Chinese society, especially among the young. "Sorry, we are the last generation, thanks!" was a popular Chinese hashtag in May 2022.[143] Now, this gloom is driving the young to turn their backs on society.[144] The University of Pennsylvania's Victor Mair put it this way: "'Lying flat,' 'Buddha whatever,' 'Kong Yijiism,' 'involution'—China today has so many memes for opting out."[145]

The Chinese people, risking their lives and leaving their country permanently, are now telling the world that China's glory days are over.

In the most powerful way possible, they are also saying that China is failing. Under these circumstances, it would not take much to push the Chinese state over the edge. The United States cutting ties would be a signal to others that they should also sever relations with Chinese parties. An American president exercising authority under either the International Emergency Economic Powers Act of 1977 or the Trading with the Enemy Act of 1917, in addition to powers granted under other statutes, can sever most ties with China. Congress can do the rest. And cutting links is necessary in any event: The United States does not want to be brought down by being tied to a China that is tumbling out of control.

Yes, Americans will feel the disruptive effects as companies move supply chains out of China. Some products will become scarce, for instance. Executives are already moving factories off Chinese soil for a multitude of reasons, especially Xi Jinping's determined assault on foreign business. Nobody should think that divorcing a predatory state will be painless.

And nobody should think opposing China in such a direct way will not be risky. Yet saying that something is risky is no longer a meaningful objection, because after decades of misguided policies, every path forward for America is risky and dangerous.

And the most risky and dangerous course of action of all is to continue with the approaches that created this precarious situation in the first place. Policies that attempt to maintain working relationships with Beijing sound "responsible" and appear as if they should work, but in fact they have not. It is now obvious that current policies will not dissuade the Communist Party from its hostile path.

In any event, it is morally and strategically wrong to continue to give a hostile regime the means to kill Americans.

China cannot attack America without American money and technology. It's about time that America stopped supplying them.

Notes

1. "Speech by Comrade Chi Haotian," ChinaAffairs.org, November 26, 2009, https://www.chinaaffairs.org/gb/detail.asp?id=99315. It is believed that the speech, which surfaced in late 2005, was delivered around the turn of the century.
2. Middle East Media Research Institute (@MEMRIReports), tweet of November 30, 2020, https://twitter.com/MEMRIReports/status/1333327936380936192.
3. William Burns, "A World Transformed and the Role of Intelligence," 59th Ditchley Annual Lecture, Charlbury, England, July 1, 2023, https://www.ditchley.com/sites/default/files/Ditchley%20Annual%20Lecture%202023%20transcript.pdf.
4. For a discussion of Xi Jinping's increasingly open efforts to export China's model, see Joshua Kurlantzick, *Beijing's Global Media Offensive:*

China's Uneven Campaign to Influence Asia and the World (New York: Oxford University Press, 2023), pp. 6–7.

5. Martin Jacques, *When China Rules the World: The End of the Western World and the Birth of a New Global Order* (New York: Penguin Press, 2009), p. 8.
6. Ibid., p. 16.
7. "Xi Pledges 'Great Renewal of Chinese Nation,'" Xinhua News Agency, November 29, 2012, http://news.xinhuanet.com/english/china/2012-11/29/c_132008231.htm.
8 *See* Gordon G. Chang, "China Shakes the World: A Revolutionary Remaking of the International Order," *Telos*, Winter 2022, p. 38, http://journal.telospress.com/content/2022/201/38.full.pdf+html.
9. An Baijie, "Xi Advocates Common Security," *China Daily* (Beijing), June 12, 2017, http://www.chinadaily.com.cn/world/2017xivisitskazakhstan/2017-06/12/content_29705208.htm.
10. Zhang Yunbi, "Fresh Vision Spurs Growth, Cooperation," *China Daily* (Beijing), August 17, 2021, http://www.chinadaily.com.cn/a/202108/17/WS611af037a310efa1bd669216.html. Moreover, Beijing has recently broadened "mankind" to all living creatures as it moves to take advantage of the biodiversity movement. "Xiplomacy"—the Communist Party is building a personality cult around its leader by combining his name with "diplomacy"—is "building a shared future for all life." *See* "Xiplomacy: Xi Promotes Global Efforts Towards Building a Shared Future for All Life," Xinhua News Agency, May 22, 2022, https://english

.news.cn/20220522/8a1a5fdc9f894541843182eeaa6d320d/c.html.

11. For more, see He Yafei, "A Paradigm Shift in Global Governance," *China Daily* (Beijing), August 7, 2017, http://www.chinadaily.com.cn/opinion/2017-08/07/content_30350545.htm.
12. Fei-Ling Wang, *The China Order: Centralia, World Empire, and the Nature of Chinese Power* (Albany: State University of New York Press, 2017), p. 211.
13. "Chairman Xi Jinping's 2017 New Year's Message," Xinhua News Agency, December 31, 2016, http://news.xinhuanet.com/politics/2016-12/31/c_1120227034.htm.
14. Ministry of Foreign Affairs, "Forge Ahead Under the Guidance of General Secretary Xi Jinping's Thought on Diplomacy," September 1, 2017, http://www.fmprc.gov.cn/mfa_eng/zxxx_662805/t1489143.shtml. For more, see "China Says Xi Transcends West as a Diplomatic 'Pioneer,'" Reuters, September 1, 2017, https://www.reuters.com/article/us-china-congress-diplomacy/china-says-xi-transcends-west-as-a-diplomatic-pioneer-idUSKCN1BC4KQ.
15. Xi Jinping, "Speech at a Ceremony Marking the Centenary of the Communist Party of China," July 1, 2021, Beijing, China, http://www.gov.cn/xinwen/2021-07/01/content_5621847.htm.
16. "Commentary: China's Worldview Rooted in Ancient Civilization," Xinhua News Agency, July 5, 2023, http://en.people.cn/n3/2023/0705/c90000-20039586.html.
17. Wang, *China Order*, p. 101.
18. Ibid., p. 100.

19. Henry Kissinger, *World Order* (New York: Penguin Books, 2014), p. 4.
20. Ibid., p. 213.
21. Henry Kissinger, *On China* (New York: Penguin Press, 2011), p. 481.
22. Howard W. French, *Everything Under the Heavens: How the Past Helps Shape China's Push for Global Power* (New York: Alfred A. Knopf, 2017), p. 12.
23. Stephen R. Platt, "The Chip on China's Shoulder," review of *Everything Under the Heavens* by Howard W. French, *Wall Street Journal*, March 24, 2017, https://www.wsj.com/articles/the-chip-on-chinas-shoulder-1490388803.
24. *See* Brendon Hong, "China's Looming Land Grab in Outer Space," Daily Beast, June 22, 2018, https://www.thedailybeast.com/chinas-looming-land-grab-in-outer-space.
25. Ibid.
26. "China's First Mars Rover Named Zhurong," Xinhua News Agency, April 24, 2021, http://www.xinhuanet.com/english/2021-04/24/c_139902817.htm.
27. Madeleine Albright with Bill Woodward, *Madam Secretary* (New York: Miramax Books, 2003), p. 506. The phrase was originally Bill Clinton's from his second inaugural address in 1997.
28. Fareed Zakaria, "'A History of Britain': The Previous Superpower," review of *A History of Britain: The Fate of Empire, 1776-2000* by Simon Schama, *New York Times Book Review*, July 27, 2003, p. 11, https://www.nytimes.com/2003/07/27/books/the-previous-superpower.html.
29. "Editorial, "American Side Keeps Shouting Arrogantly, In Fact It's Self-Motivation," *People's*

Daily (Beijing), May 13, 2019, http://opinion.people.com.cn/n1/2019/0513/c1003-31082607.html.

30. Jack Lau, "China's Military Urged to Keep Focus on Active Defense in Fighting a 'People's War,'" *South China Morning Post* (Hong Kong), April 1, 2023, https://scmp.com/news/china/military/article/3215616/chinas-military-urged-keep-focus-active-defence-fighting-peoples-war.
31. John Garnaut, "China's Power Politics," *New York Times*, August 11, 2014, http://www.nytimes.com/2014/08/12/opinion/chinas-power-politics.html?partner=rss&emc=rss&_r=1.
32. *See, e.g.*, Shannon Tiezzi, "In Xi's 'New Era,' China's Foreign Policy Centers on 'Struggle,' " Diplomat, March 8, 2023, https://thediplomat.com/2023/03/in-xis-new-era-chinas-foreign-policy-centers-on-struggle/.
33. Kerry Gershaneck, email message to author, July 9, 2023.
34. Michael Pillsbury, *The Hundred-Year Marathon: China's Secret Strategy to Replace America as the Global Superpower* (New York: Henry Holt, 2015), p. 12.
35. Ibid., p. 235.
36. Ibid., p. 236.
37. Francis Fukuyama, "History and September 11," in *Worlds in Collision: Terror and the Future of Global Order*, pp. 27–36 (Basingstoke, England: Palgrave Macmillan, 2002).
38. Francis Fukuyama, "The End of History?" *National Interest*, Summer 1989, p. 3.
39. Robert B. Zoellick, "Remarks to National Committee on U.S.-China Relations," New York City, September

21, 2005, https://2001-2009.state.gov/s/d/former/zoellick/rem/53682.htm.

40. Pillsbury, *The Hundred-Year Marathon*, p. 32.
41. Ibid., p. 19.
42. Ibid., p. 4.
43. Ibid., p. 45.
44. Biden, in May 2023, called the object "this silly balloon." "Biden Predicts 'Imminent Thaw' with China, Mocks 'Silly Balloon,'" Newsmax, May 21, 2023, https://www.newsmax.com/newsfront/joe-biden-china-balloon/2023/05/21/id/1120615/.
45. "Xi Urged China Military in 2020 to Brace for War Amid West's Decline," Kyodo News, July 24, 2023, https://english.kyodonews.net/news/2023/07/01bb652a507f-xi-urged-china-military-in-2020-to-brace-for-war-amid-wests-decline.html.
46. Al Jazeera Newsfeed, "Xi Tells Putin of 'Changes Not Seen for 100 Years,'" YouTube, March 22, 2023, https://www.youtube.com/watch?v=bEpTRr7QcWg.
47. Brooke Singman, "China's Anti-Trump Election Meddling Raises New Alarm, as DNI Calls Country Biggest Threat," Fox News, August 17, 2020, https://www.foxnews.com/politics/china-election-interference-threat.
48. In late January 2020—just months before the George Floyd protests—U.S. Customs and Border Protection agents in the International Falls Port of Entry in Minnesota seized 900,000 counterfeit $1 bills made in China. See Francisco Guzman and Brian Ries, "Customs Police Seized $900,000 in Counterfeit Money from a Shipping Container—All in $1 Bills," CNN, January 28, 2020, https://www.cnn.com/2020/01/28/us/cbp-seized-shipping-container-trnd/index.html. Nobody, in China's

near-total surveillance state can counterfeit American currency without authorities knowing about it, so this counterfeiting operation, in all probability, had Beijing's blessing. We do not know the motive for this operation, but it could not have been for profit. Yet, whatever the reason, counterfeiting another country's currency is considered an act of war. In May 2020, U.S. authorities in Louisville seized 10,800 assault weapons parts smuggled in from China. *See* "10,800 Assault Weapons Parts Seized by CBP in Louisville," U.S. Customs and Border Protection, June 26, 2020, https://www.cbp.gov/newsroom/local-media-release/10800-assault-weapons-parts-seized-cbp-louisville. Those who sent the parts were probably attempting to promote violence. More recently, Chinese parties are exporting to the U.S. "Glock switches," which convert handguns into fully automatic weapons. *See* Rebecca Robinson, "China Flooding US with Deadly 'Glock Switches' to Spark Violence on the Streets—Claim," Daily Express US, February 26, 2024, https://www.the-express.com/news/world-news/129137/china-glock-switches-destabilize-america.

49. *See* Edward Wong, Matthew Rosenberg, and Julian E. Barnes, "Chinese Agents Helped Spread Messages that Sowed Virus Panic in U.S., Officials Say," *New York Times*, April 22, 2020, https://www.nytimes.com/2020/04/22/us/politics/coronavirus-china-disinformation.html. For more information on China's efforts, see Li Yuan, "With Selective Coronavirus Coverage, China Builds a Culture of Hate," *New York Times*, April 22, 2020, https://www.nytimes.com/2020/04/22/business/china-coronavirus-propaganda.html.

50. *See* Chris Ciaccia, "President Trump Targeted in Videos from Chinese Network of Fake Accounts, as Big Tech Battles Back," Fox News, August 13, 2020, https://www.foxnews.com/tech/big-tech-fighting-back-against-chinese-network-fake-accounts-targeting-trump.
51. Robert McMillan, "Twitter Purges 174,000 Fake Accounts Linked to Chinese Government," Market Watch, June 11, 2020, https://www.marketwatch.com/story/twitter-purges-174000-fake-accounts-linked-to-chinese-government-2020-06-11.
52. Paul Dabrowa, email message to author, July 31, 2020.
53. Kerry Gershaneck, email message to author, July 9, 2023.
54. Cleo Paskal, email message to author, July 27, 2023.
55. *See, e.g.*, "The 'Everything App' for China's Journalists," China Media Project, July 4, 2023, https://chinamediaproject.org/2023/07/04/the-new-everything-app/.
56. Don Neuen and Donna Fiducia, telephone conference with author, July 15, 2023.
57. Valeria Ricciulli, "How the Young Lords Brought the Revolution to Drug Treatment," Curbed, October 25, 2021, https://www.curbed.com/2021/10/young-lords-acupuncture-detox-bronx-lincoln-hospital.html.
58. Cleo Paskal, email message to author, July 27, 2023.
59. Chen Weihua (@chenweihua), tweet of October 18, 2021, https://twitter.com/chenweihua/status/1317792465286516738.
60. *See* "Chinese Consulate in Houston Intervened in US Political Movement," Chinascope, August 18, 2020, http://chinascope.org/archives/24225.

61. Brandon Weichert, email message to author, March 27, 2023.
62. Paul Dabrowa, telephone conference with author, August 7, 2020.
63. Keith Krach, WhatsApp message to author, March 20, 2023.
64. *See* Thomas Burrows, "How TikTok Has Become a Hotbed for Drug Users Who Teach Kids How to Take Class As," *U.S. Sun*, February 29, 2020, https://www.the-sun.com/news/470759/how-tiktok-has-become-a-hotbed-for-drug-users-who-teach-kids-how-to-take-class-as/.
65. Kerry Gershaneck, email message to author, March 21, 2022.
66. Kerry Gershaneck, email message to author, July 9, 2023.
67. *See* Steven Nelson, "Joe Biden Got $40K from China Funds, Brother James Admits in Bombshell Impeachment Interview," *New York Post*, March 1, 2024, https://nypost.com/2024/03/01/us-news/joe-biden-got-40k-in-china-funds-brother-james-admits-in-bombshell-impeachment-interview/.
68. *See* Victor Nava, "Where the Money Went: The Bidens and Biden Associates Who Received Chinese Cash," *New York Post*, March 17, 2023, https://nypost.com/2023/03/17/where-the-money-went-the-bidens-and-biden-associates-that-received-chinese-cash/; Annie Grayer, "House GOP Digs In on China-Linked Payments to Biden Family Members in New Memo," CNN, March 17, 2023, https://www.cnn.com/2023/03/16/politics/house-gop-memo-biden-family/index.html.
69. *See* James Gordon, "Trump Tweets Video of Chinese Professor Claiming That Beijing Can

Swing US Policy Because It Has 'People at the Top of America's Core Inner Circle of Power' in Clip That Has Been Deleted from Social Media in China," *Daily Mail* (London), December 8, 2020, https://www.dailymail.co.uk/news/article-9029383/Trump-tweets-video-Chinese-professor-claiming-Beijing-swing-policy.html.

70. *See* Aaron Navarro, "Biden Reelection Campaign Joins TikTok—Though Biden Banned Its Use on Government Devices," CBS News, February 12, 2024, https://www.cbsnews.com/news/biden-campaign-joins-tiktok-though-biden-banned-use-on-government-devices/.
71. *See*, *e.g.*, Bethany Allen and Zach Dorfman, "Exclusive: Suspected Chinese Spy Targeted California Politicians," Axios, December 8, 2020, https://www.axios.com/2020/12/08/china-spy-california-politicians.
72. Charles Burton, email message to author, July 8, 2023.
73. Ibid.
74. *See* Jimmy Quinn, "Group That Hosted New York's Chinese Police Station Celebrates July 4," National Review Online, July 7, 2023, https://www.nationalreview.com/2023/07/group-that-hosted-new-yorks-chinese-police-station-celebrates-july-4/.
75. Jane Tang, "'Secret' New York Police Station Is Mere Sliver of Beijing's U.S. Harassment Push," Radio Free Asia, July 7, 2023, https://www.rfa.org/english/news/special/nyc-police-chinese/index.html.
76. *See* Philip Lenczycki, "EXCLUSIVE: GOP Senators Demand Biden DOJ Provide Answers on CCP Intel-Linked 'Service Centers,'" Daily Caller News Foundation, July 10, 2023, https://dailycaller.com/

2023/07/10/ccp-service-centers-ufwd-lawmakers/?pnespid=vb5gVCZaMr8e1anRtDC7TZ2Q5hn0TYB_P7O2kOtrp0Zmp4nLf.mq4WrPyIkoRV..u4YxVADa.

77. *See* Isabel Vincent, "After FBI Busts Chinese 'Police Stations' in NYC, Six More Exposed in US," *New York Post*, April 18, 2023, https://nypost.com/2023/04/18/chinese-police-stations-allegedly-spying-on-nyc-la-more/.
78. Kerry Gershaneck, email message to author, July 9, 2023.
79. *See* Liu Caiyu and Fan Anqi, "More Evidence Supports Multiple Virus Origins," *Global Times* (Beijing), November 29, 2020, https://www.globaltimes.cn/content/1208404.shtml.
80. *See, e.g.*, Nicholas Wade, "Where Did Covid Come From?" *Wall Street Journal*, February 28, 2024, https://www.wsj.com/articles/where-did-covid-come-from-new-evidence-lab-leak-hypothesis-78be1c39.
81. Sean Lin, email message to author, February 2, 2021.
82. Wang Xiaodong, "Top Expert: Disease Spread Won't Be on Scale of SARS," *China Daily* (Beijing), January 21, 2020, http://www.chinadaily.com.cn/a/202001/21/WS5e25f635a31012821727256a.html.
83. "WHO Statement Regarding Cluster of Pneumonia Cases in Wuhan, China," World Health Organization, January 9, 2020, https://www.who.int/china/news/detail/09-01-2020-who-statement-regarding-cluster-of-pneumonia-cases-in-wuhan-china.

84. World Health Organization (WHO) (@WHO), tweet of January 14, 2020, https://twitter.com/who/status/1217043229427761152?lang=en.
85. *See, e.g.*, Lawrence Wright, "The Plague Year," *New Yorker*, December 28, 2020, https://www.newyorker.com/magazine/2021/01/04/the-plague-year.
86. COVID Data Tracker, Centers for Disease Control and Prevention, https://covid.cdc.gov/covid-data-tracker/#datatracker-home.
87. Elsa B. Kania and Wilson VornDick, "Under Beijing's Civil-Military Fusion Strategy, the PLA Is Sponsoring Research on Gene Editing, Human Performance Enhancement, and More," Defense One, August 14, 2019, https://www.defenseone.com/ideas/2019/08/chinas-military-pursuing-biotech/159167/.
88. Bill Gertz, "China Deception Fuels Fears of Biological Weapons Ethnic Experiments," *Washington Times*, May 14, 2020, https://m.washingtontimes.com/news/2020/may/14/china-deception-fuels-fears-biological-weapons-eth/.
89. Richard D. Fisher, Jr., email message to author, July 3, 2023.
90. Cleo Paskal, email message to author, January 31, 2021.
91. *See* Geoff Mulvihill, "China's Agreement Expected to Slow Flow of Fentanyl into US, but Not Solve Overdose Epidemic," Associated Press, November 16, 2023, https://apnews.com/article/biden-xi-fentanyl-agreement-mexico-china-opioids-1fa57facd0dbdac714b616d705952d92.
92. *See* White House, "Statement by National Security Council Spokesperson Ned Price on U.S.-China Enhanced Control Measures for Fentanyl,"

September 3, 2016, https://obamawhitehouse.archives.gov/the-press-office/2016/09/03/statement-national-security-council-spokesperson-ned-price-us-china.

93. *See* "Select Committee Unveils Findings into CCP's Role in American Fentanyl Epidemic—REPORT & HEARING," House Select Committee on the Chinese Communist Party, April 16, 2024, https://selectcommitteeontheccp.house.gov/media/press-releases/select-committee-unveils-findings-ccps-role-american-fentanyl-epidemic-report.
94. Vanda Felbab-Brown, "Fentanyl and Geopolitics: Controlling Opioid Supply from China," Brookings Institution, July 2020, https://www.brookings.edu/wp-content/uploads/2020/07/8_Felbab-Brown_China_final.pdf.
95. Anthony Ruggiero, "China in Our Backyard: How Chinese Money Laundering Organizations Enrich the Cartels," testimony before the Subcommittee on Health Care and Financial Services of the House Oversight and Accountability Committee, April 26, 2023, https://oversight.house.gov/wp-content/uploads/2023/04/04-26-23-Ruggiero-Written-Testimony-FINAL.pdf.
96. *See* Simon Kemp, "Digital 2024: China," Datareportal, February 21, 2024, https://datareportal.com/reports/digital-2024-china.
97. Ministry of Foreign Affairs of the People's Republic of China, "Foreign Ministry Spokesperson Mao Ning's Regular Press Conference on April 6, 2023," April 6, 2023, https://www.fmprc.gov.cn/eng/xwfw_665399/s2510_665401/2511_665403/202304/t20230406_11055468.html.

98. Darzen Jorgic, “Special Report: Burner Phones and Banking Apps: Meet the Chinese ‘Brokers’ Laundering Mexican Drug Money,” Reuters, December 3, 2020, https://www.reuters.com/article/us-mexico-china-cartels-specialreport/special-report-burner-phones-and-banking-apps-meet-the-chinese-brokers-laundering-mexican-drug-money-idUSKBN28D1M4.
99. Jeff Seldin, “Top US Commander Warns ‘Front Line’ with China Now South of Border,” Voice of America, March 16, 2021, https://www.voanews.com/a/americas_top-us-commander-warns-front-line-china-now-south-border/6203386.html.
100. Joe Leahy, Kathrin Hille, Andy Lin, and Michael Pooler, “‘Dare to Fight’: Xi Jinping Unveils China’s New World Order,” *Financial Times* (London), March 31, 2023, https://www.ft.com/content/0f0b558b-3ca8-4156-82c8-e1825539ee20.
101. *See* Zhao Lei, “Military Urged to Strengthen Innovation,” *China Daily* (Beijing), March 8, 2024, http://www.chinadaily.com.cn/a/202403/08/WS65ea48b4a31082fc043bb501.html.
102. *See* Bryce Moore, “Chinese Satellite Beams Green Lasers Over Hawaii,” *Hill*, February 13, 2023, https://thehill.com/policy/technology/3854939-chinese-satellite-beams-green-lasers-over-hawaii/.
103. Richard D. Fisher, Jr, email message to author, February 13, 2023.
104. *See, e.g.*, Kylie Atwood, “China Is Giving Russia Significant Support to Expand Weapons Manufacturing as Ukraine War Continues, US Officials Say,” CNN, April 12, 2024, https://www.cnn.com/2024/04/12/politics/china-russia-support-weapons-manufacturing/index.html.

Secretary of State Antony Blinken defined "lethal" in early 2023. *See* Craig Howie, "Blinken: 'Deep Concern' that China Could Provide Lethal Support for Russia's War in Ukraine," Politico, February 18, 2023, https://www.politico.com/news/2023/02/18/blinken-china-russia-war-ukraine-00083577.

105. *See* Ryosuke Hanafusa, Shuntaro Fukutomi, and Yuta Koga, "Iran's Oil Exports Reach 5-Year High, with China as Top Buyer," Nikkei Asia, January 31, 2024, https://asia.nikkei.com/Business/Markets/Commodities/Iran-s-oil-exports-reach-5-year-high-with-China-as-top-buyer.

106. *See, e.g.*, "TV Report: Huge Quantities of Chinese-Made Weapons Being Used by Hamas in Gaza," Times of Israel, December 30, 2023, https://www.timesofisrael.com/liveblog_entry/tv-report-huge-quantities-of-chinese-made-weapons-being-used-by-hamas-in-gaza/.

107. *See, e.g.*, "Lebanon's Hezbollah: What Weapons Does It Have?" Reuters, October 30, 2023, https://www.reuters.com/world/middle-east/lebanons-hezbollah-what-weapons-does-it-have-2023-10-30/.

108. *See, e.g.*, Lloyd Lee, "Here's What Nearly 10,000 Rifles, 200 Rocket Launchers, and Nearly 800,000 Rounds of Ammunition and Other Weapons Seized by the US Government Looks Like," *Business Insider*, July 15, 2023, https://www.businessinsider.com/photos-us-seized-10k-rifles-800k-pounds-ammunition-yemen-iran-2023-7?amp.

109. China and Russia have been constantly engaged in joint exercises, and many of them look like they target Japan. *See, e.g.*, "Russia, China End Military

Exercises in Sea of Japan," Voice of America, July 23, 2023," https://www.voanews.com/a/russia-china-end-military-exercises-in-sea-of-japan/7192837.html.

110. North Korean propaganda has recently been suggesting it would go to war over Taiwan. *See, e.g.*, Soo-Hyang Choi, "North Korea Denounces US Arms Aid to Taiwan as 'Dangerous Provocation,'" Reuters, August 4, 2023, https://www.reuters.com/world/asia-pacific/north-korea-denounces-us-arms-aid-taiwan-dangerous-provocation-2023-08-03/?fbclid=IwAR39llrsArwZJMHDa7qpsAAoL3x6UT5u9Au_hq88FDSj0KRu7QqmzdBA-iE.

111. Richard D. Fisher, Jr, email message to author, July 29, 2023.

112. James Fanell, email message to author, July 29, 2023.

113. *See* Zachary Keck, "State Media Boasts of China's Ability to Nuke US Cities," Diplomat, November 5, 2013, https://thediplomat.com/2013/11/state-media-boasts-of-chinas-ability-to-nuke-us-cities/.

114. "Chinese Defense Spokesperson: Australia Has No Business Interfering Taiwan Question," China Military Online, March 13, 2022, http://eng.chinamil.com.cn/BILINGUAL/News_209203/10140066.html.

115. Richard D. Fisher, Jr, email message to author, February 28, 2024.

116. Corey Dickstein, "Air Force Secretary Labels China's Rapid Nuclear Expansion Most 'Disturbing' Threat He Has Seen," *Stars and Stripes*, March 28, 2023, https://www.stripes.com/branches/air_force/2023-03-28/air-force-china-nuclear-weapons-9634406.html.

117. *See, e.g.*, Gordon G. Chang, "Is China Sparking Stealth War in the Air?" *Hill*, June 8, 2022, https://thehill.com/opinion/national-security/3515654-is-china-sparking-stealth-war-in-the-air/.
118. James Fanell, email message to author, June 5, 2022.
119. *See* Richard Sisk, "US Complains After Chinese Lasers Injures 2 Air Force Pilots in Africa," Military.com, May 3, 2018, https://www.military.com/defensetech/2018/05/03/us-complains-after-chinese-lasers-injure-2-air-force-pilots-africa.html.
120. *See* William La Jeunesse and Lee Ross, "Cleanup at Suspicious California Biolab with Ties to China Continues," Fox News, January 18, 2024, https://www.foxnews.com/us/cleanup-suspicious-california-biolab-ties-china-finally-underway; Doha Madani, "CDC Detects Coronavirus, HIV, Hepatitis and Herpes at Unlicensed California Lab," NBC News, July 27, 2023, https://www.nbcnews.com/news/us-news/officials-believe-fresno-warehouse-was-site-illegal-laboratory-rcna96756.
121. Katy Grimes, "Mysterious Chinese COVID Lab Uncovered in City of Reedley CA," California Globe, July 28, 2023, https://californiaglobe.com/articles/mysterious-chinese-covid-lab-uncovered-in-city-of-reedly-ca/.
122. The activities at the Reedley lab are not the only indications that China is contemplating biological attacks on America. In 2020, parties in China sent, unsolicited, seeds to Americans in all 50 states. It appears that Beijing was attempting to introduce invasive species into the United States, a form of biological or ecological warfare. *See, e.g.*, Gordon

G. Chang, "China Seeds: A Biological Attack on America?" Gatestone Institute, July 30, 2020, https://www.gatestoneinstitute.org/16293/china-seeds-biological-attack.

123. Brandon Weichert, email message to author, August 1, 2023.
124. Michael Yon, WhatsApp message to author, June 26, 2023.
125. *See* Sharyn Alfonsi, "Chinese Migrants Are the Fastest Growing Group Crossing from Mexico into U.S. at Southern Border," CBS News, February 4, 2024, https://www.cbsnews.com/news/chinese-migrants-fastest-growing-group-us-mexico-border-60-minutes-transcript/. For additional information, see Aline Barros and Tracy Wen Liu, "Growing Number of Migrants from China Arriving at US-Mexico Border," Voice of America, April 13, 2023, https://www.voanews.com/a/growing-number-of-migrants-from-china-arriving-at-us-mexico-border-/7049608.html.
126. Stephen Dinan, "China Likely Exploiting Border Chaos to Sneak Military Operatives into U.S.: House Chairman," *Washington Times*, June 14, 2023, https://www.washingtontimes.com/news/2023/jun/14/chinese-may-be-inserting-military-operatives-throu/.
127. Michael Yon, WhatsApp message to author, June 26, 2023.
128. Ibid.
129. *See* Mack Cogburn, "Videos from Chinese Illegals That Entered Our Country Three Weeks Ago Seems [sic] to Show That They Are Entitled to the Second Amendment," Defiant America, January 12, 2024, https://defiantamerica.com/videos-from

-chinese-illegals-that-entered-our-country-three-weeks-ago-seems-to-show-that-they-are-entitled-to-the-second-amendment/.

130. Blaine Holt, email message to author, February 8, 2024. For more, see Gordon G. Chang, "China's Infiltrators: 'They Are Coming Here to Kill Us,'" Gatestone Institute, February 13, 2024, https://www.gatestoneinstitute.org/20388/china-infiltrators-us.

131. In February 2024, three Chinese nationals tried to sneak into Maine from Canada under cover of darkness. A fourth Chinese national from New York was waiting in a car on the U.S. side of the border. There is, apparently, a network of Chinese in the U.S. involved in aiding illegal entries. The three individuals, attempting to avoid detection, were obviously not seeking asylum. *See* Lawrence Richard and Bill Melugin, "Northern Border: Agents Arrest Group of Chinese Trying to Sneak into Maine from Canada," Fox News, February 29, 2024, https://www.foxnews.com/us/northern-border-agents-arrest-group-chinese-trying-sneak-into-maine-from-canada.

132. *See* Tom Vanden Brook, "Suspected Chinese Spies, Disguised as Tourists, Try to Infiltrate Alaskan Military Bases," *USA Today*, May 31, 2023, https://www.usatoday.com/story/news/politics/2023/05/31/suspected-chinese-spies-posing-as-tourists-discovered-in-alaska/70260712007/.

133. Richard D. Fisher, Jr, email message to author, June 27, 2023.

134. *See* Gordon, "Trump Tweets Video of Chinese Professor Claiming That Beijing Can Swing US Policy Because It Has 'People at the Top of

America's Core Inner Circle of Power' in Clip That Has Been Deleted from Social Media in China."

135. China Observer, "Di Dongsheng 1: We have People at the Top of America's Circle-2020," YouTube video, December 8, 2020, https://youtu.be/Df1ViazTCn0?si=wNBnTju2dZGjNKu2.
136. Jeffrey Rodack, "Tesla Signs Pledge to Promote 'Core Socialist Values,'" Newsmax, July 7, 2023, https://www.newsmax.com/newsfront/musk-tesla-china/2023/07/07/id/1126336/; Edward White, Gloria Li, and Qianer Liu, "Tesla and Chinese Rivals Signal EV Price War Truce in 'Socialist Values' Pledge," *Financial Times* (London), July 5, 2023, https://www.ft.com/content/6e08ea9b-0c4a-4e0f-8a13-0eca06aa76b9.
137. Oren Cass and Gabriela Rodriguez, "The Case for a Hard Break with China," *Foreign Affairs*, July 25, 2023, https://www.foreignaffairs.com/china/case-for-hard-break-with-beijing-economic-derisking?utm_medium=promo_email&utm_source=lo_flows&utm_campaign=registered_user_welcome&utm_term=email_1&utm_content=20230729 .
138. Christopher Wray, "The Threat Posed by the Chinese Government and the Chinese Communist Party to the Economic and National Security of the United States," Hudson Institute, Washington, D.C., July 7, 2020, https://www.fbi.gov/news/speeches/the-threat-posed-by-the-chinese-government-and-the-chinese-communist-party-to-the-economic-and-national-security-of-the-united-states.
139. "Xi Focus: Xi Stresses Racing Against Time to Reach Chinese Dream," Xinhua News Agency, January 23,

2020, http://www.xinhuanet.com/english/2020-01/23/c_138729706.htm.

140. Beijing reported that China's population was 1.41 billion at the end of 2022, which, according to official statistics, was the first year of population decline since 1961. Everyone agrees that China will continue to shrink. Projections issued by the U.N.'s World Population Prospects 2022 show a high variant estimate for 2100 of 1.15 billion people. The high variant, based on Beijing's numbers, is unrealistic. The low variant—the most realistic estimate from all indications—is 487.93 billion. The U.N.'s low number has dropped precipitously: It was 684.05 million in its 2019 estimates. Even the 2022 low variant might be too high. Demographers from Xian Jiaotong University in 2021 estimated that the number of people could fall by 50 percent in five decades. *See* Stephen Chen, "China's Population Could Halve Within the Next 45 Years, New Study Warns," *South China Morning Post* (Hong Kong), September 30, 2021, https://www.scmp.com/news/china/science/article/3150699/chinas-population-could-halve-within-next-45-years-new-study. This projection assumes that the country maintains a Total Fertility Rate—generally the average number of children per female reaching child-bearing age—of 1.3. China's TFR, according to official sources, was 1.18 in 2022. Some demographers believe it is as low as 0.9.

141. Peter Huessy, email message to author, April 1, 2023.

142. *See* Haley Ott, Elizabeth Palmer, and Shuai Zhang, "China's Xi Jinping Faces Calls to Step Down as Deadly Fire Sparks Unprecedented Protests Over

'Zero-COVID' Policy," CBS News, November 28, 2022, https://www.cbsnews.com/news/xi-jinping-step-down-china-deadly-fire-protests-zero-covid-policy/.

143. *See* Cheryl Teh, "'We Are the Last Generation': China's Youth Rallied Around a Now-Censored Social Media Hashtag to Rage About Their Disillusionment with Life and Disdain at Draconian Lockdowns," Yahoo! News, May 25, 2022, https://www.yahoo.com/news/last-generation-chinas-youth-rallied-090029327.html?guccounter=1.
144. *See* Ivana Davidovic, "'Lying Flat': Why Some Chinese Are Putting Work Second," BBC News, February 16, 2022, https://www.bbc.com/news/business-60353916.
145. Victor Mair, "The Growing Supinity of Chinese Youth," Language Log, July 11, 2023, https://languagelog.ldc.upenn.edu/nll/?p=59648.

INDEX

ABOUT THE AUTHOR

GORDON G. CHANG lived and worked in Shanghai and Hong Kong for almost two decades. He is a columnist at *Newsweek*, a regular contributor to *The Hill*, and writes for Newsmax. His writings have appeared in *The New York Times*, *The Wall Street Journal*, *National Review*, *The American Conservative*, *Commentary*, *Barron's*, and The Daily Beast. He is the author of *China Is Going to War*, *The Great U.S.-China Tech War*, *Losing South Korea*, *Nuclear Showdown: North Korea Takes On the World*, and *The Coming Collapse of China*.

Visit the author at GordonChang.com. Follow him on X @GordonGChang.